# Mediterranean Houses
# Italy

**Editorial Gustavo Gili, S.A.**

**08029 Barcelona** Rosselló, 87-89
Spain
Tel. (343) 322 81 61   Fax (343) 322 92 05

# Mediterranean Houses Italy

**Giovanni Albera/Nicolas Monti**

**GG**®

## Acknowledgments

In producing this book, we are indebted to several people. Our appreciation is extended to the architects and their collaborators, the photographers and the owners who made their work and property available for the preparation of this book and for services rendered.

Special thanks go to Elena Elli and Cristina Colombo for their help in the initial research for the book. Special thanks are also extended to the following for the information they provided: Francesco Garofalo, Adriana Monti, Giorgio Muratore, Ettore Pellegrini, Alberto Scarzella.

Many thanks for their support and special assistance to the following individuals: Davide Riva, Roberta Bernasconi.

For reading the manuscript, discussing our ideas and offering most helpful advice we are much inebted to Franca Fava and Ferdinando Monti. We are also deeply grateful to our editor, Mònica Gili, for her patience with our delays and understanding of our difficulties in collecting the material and her great skill in putting this book together

**Translation:** Graham Thomson

© Editorial Gustavo Gili, S.A., Barcelona, 1992

ISBN: 84-252-1524-2
Depósito legal: B. 30.906-1992
Printed in Spain by Grafos, S. A. Arte sobre papel

# Contents

# Introduction

The landscape of Europe, and in particular that of Italy, is to a great extent an expression of culture, the product of constant and indefatigable human intervention, developed and stratified over the course of centuries.

This is a land in which one is never alone; mutable in its beauty, the panorama permanently retains a human quality. Here, nature is irremediably domesticated. Stripped of its gloomy forests, overlaid with the geometry of cultivation, cut into terraces and worked to the very tops of the hills, the panorama has been profoundly modelled by the work of human hands. Every bay shelters its fishing village or its port; every promontory, however forgotten and remote, conceals the ruins of some secular building; on every hillside the country people have laid out a vineyard or a well-tended field; a belltower rises up from every clump of pines.

Accordingly, the preexisting elements which the architect has to confront are almost always highly structured. Over and above its natural morphology, the terrain is strongly characterized by the densely layered traces of a thousand years of history and a great diversity of different civilizations, each one leaving behind its indelible mark. The omnipresent beauties of nature and art both stimulate and complicate every new intervention. The cultural antiquity of the old continent presents the contemporary architect with particularly acute problems; with the conflict between respect for and impatience with a historical heritage that is at once too evident and too diffuse.

For thousands of years the coasts of Italy have been a privileged place of encounter/ conflict between societies and cultures adhering to highly differentiated models (we need look no further than the contrasts between the continental and the insular mentality).

It would, then, be easy to conclude that there is in Italy no such thing as a "Mediterranean" architecture that can be defined as typical, with uniform, unitary features. That it would be more appropriate to seek to define a collection of architectures in possession of certain common, shared characteristics. To some extent this situation can be attributed to a certain numerical predominance of Milanese architects; a fact that inevitably reflects the source of the majority of clients and commissions. Amongst the best and the worst are the little bits of Milan constructed at considerable distances from Milan for people from Milan, who occupy them only during holidays.

Creativity and rationality find in architecture a fertile locus of encounter and, at least up until a few years ago, Milan represented the synthesis of these often opposing qualities which have made Italy unique. Milan's geographical location, too, equally close to both the Alps and the Mediterranean, seems to make it ideally suitable as a point of encounter, combining Latin sophistication and sensuality with the rigour of mid-European industrial culture.

Although culturally close to Central Europe, sharing its organized vision of life, but at the same time clearly influenced by a creative component that is typically Mediterranean, this architecture does not allow itself to be labelled easily. It is the product of intuitions and energies which are all possessed of a dual nature. It is thus quite naturally the synthesis and expression of two different spirits: a concern with the perfect functioning of the "machine house", counterpointed by a passionate concern with culture. The houses which derive from it are the expression of a way of life that is modern and highly evolved; at once rigorously rational and exceptionally refined.

These features are common to many of the houses selected for inclusion here, irrespective of their geographical location.

There are very few (fortunately or unfortunately?) cases of the modern inserted into the old. Old villages have been out of fashion as places for a holiday home for a quite some time. This is true not only of traditional houses, with their lack of modern comforts, but of the whole environment, which has come to seem unattractive because of the difficulties of getting to them and around them by car, the lack of space for the indispensable garden, swimming pool, tennis court, etc., and not least because the social make-up of the village has little to appeal to those who can afford a second home. To say nothing of the fact that it is less expensive to build a new house than refurbish an old one.

The years around the turn of the century saw the emergence of a typology (the holiday house) set apart from the urban nucleus, often a long way from the traditional centres of population, but generally fairly respectful of the landscape and the natural environment. This lasted until the postwar years.

When, starting in the sixties, even the old towns began to be fashionable, it was fashion itself (together with the conservation-mindedness reflected in the change in building regulations) which impeded new building in an already existing urban context. To offset this, during those same years from the 50s to the 70s, there was a more than compensatory growth in the area of new residential developments, to the extent that it shackled the country's coastline with a chain of concrete.

In a number of regions, this unrestrained speculation was followed by a swing to the other extreme and the introduction of severely restrictive planning regulations, leading not only to a virtually total blockage on all new building, but even on conversions or refurbishments, freezing the situation as it stood at that point in time with all its defects. In other regions, by contrast, the madness continued unabated and, unprotected by regulations and restrictions, the coasts were completely concreted over.

It is hardly surprising, then, that an extremely extensive geographical area (over 7,000 kilometres of coastline) should offer, unfortunately, a very restricted area of choice, particularly for houses built in the last few years.

Where construction has continued, the results have generally been of the poorest architectonic quality. We ought not to forget that regulations based on respect for a local architecture that frequently does not exist have abetted, if not actually imposed, the invasion of a complacently reassuring vernacular style. What this immediately brings to mind is the property development of the Costa Smeralda.

The proliferation of the banal and of decorative effusiveness was frequently founded on the convenient pretext of respect for and integration into the landscape, and on the cult of spontaneity in architecture. The immersion in the rustic, the dream of a return to tradition, these would of necessity result in an archetype of the Mediterranean house.

All along the coastline there was a crowding together and superimposing of the most heterogeneous interventions, predominantly of residential developments. These were the consequence of a period in the history of planning in which this was limited to establishing quantitative norms and standards without entering into considerations of the quality of the formal appearance, ignoring the impact on the surroundings and giving free rein to the whims of architect and client in the matter of determining what the building should actually look like. A qualititatively undistinguished and ambiguous context, the generally constrained dimensions of the site, the restrictive planning regulations, have together conspired to place obstacles in the path of any change for the better. In many parts of the country the situation has become so irrevocably compromised that the architect's concern is now to shut out the surrounding devastation, privileging all the more any remaining prospect of the sea, as in the case of the villa designed by Studio Transit, which hides itself away from its disagreeable neighbours behind a high wall (suspicious houses).

Others, as exemplified by Matteini's villas on the Romagna's riviera, take on the difficult task of showing the way forward to a possible restoration of quality to the area (protagonistic houses).

But perhaps we can do no more than wait, and hope for the consolation suggested by Delacroix: "All that man builds is, as he is, ephemeral; time lies in wait and destroys the palaces, fills in the canals, erases history..." (Eugene Delacroix, *Fragments metaphisiques,* September 21st, 1854).

Restoration schemes for the refurbishment of old buildings have not been included in the present selection, and although some of the houses considered here incorporate elements of preexisting buildings, the transformations carried out by the architects are sufficiently radical for these projects to be regarded as new constructions rather than adaptations of old buildings. The projects by Beccu, Desideri & Raimondo; Melluso & Ministeri; Salvati & Tresoldi; Tusquets & Clotet all evidence a respect for the existing, and not only complete it through their use of forms and materials that are in places modern, but their interventions are extensive enough and recognizable enough for the result to be an entirely new organism. At the same time, the selection features two restorations of the "modern" architecture which typified prewar Italian rationalism. The first, a scheme by Panero for a villa by Daneri, goes to great lengths to replicate the smallest details of the original project; while the second, in treating a villa by Ponti, skilfully exploits the incompleteness of the documentation of the period as a means to achieving greater freedom of interpretation.

Almost the diametrically opposite approach has been followed by certain other architects who, although not engaged in refurbishing existing constructions, make far from conventional use of traditional typological elements and ways of building. Indeed, was it not Ernesto Nathan Rogers, one of the founders of Italian rationalism, who asserted that "there is no truly modern work that does not have genuine roots in tradition"? (Ernesto N. Rogers, in Casabella, n.º 199, 1954)

There is much that is instructive and stimulating, even in terms of formal invention, in the ways in which local architectonic traditions, spontaneous and heavily influenced by the nature of the place, have set about confronting problems of every kind. Almost any farmhouse provides a good example of the skill of the anonymous builders in exploiting the characteristics and strengths of the site, the prevailing climatic conditions and the topography of the terrain, ably managing to resolve the relationships with the context.

The influence of rural architecture, with its enormous range of regional variants, is particularly strong, constituting a valuable heritage, above all with regard to houses and other buildings from the sphere of rural daily life, firmly rooted in the soil and tending to turn its back on the nearby sea.

Contemporary architects have widely diverse ways of drawing on this heritage. These range from Magistretti's minimal allusions, limited to the use of ornamental detail and materials borrowed from the traditional architecture of Liguria, to the recovery and at times the highlighting of a particular element (we are thinking here of the belvedere terrace of the Ilardo house, or the pergola in the villa by Papi in Forte dei Marmi), through to the adoption of a typological and structural model, as in the project by Menghi, inspired by the "magazzini" built by the country people to store their agricultural implements.

At all events, the degree of influence exerted by the local heritage can vary enormously: on the islands it was conserved virtually intact up until the last decades; this has not been the case with the Ligurian or Romagnan rivieras, even if certain typical elements of the local architecture, particularly materials, are still being used today.

However, it is very much a feature of the architecture of our own time, and in particular of the seasonal holiday home, to build on sites which our ancestors considered unsuitable for any lasting settlement. Excellent examples of this are certain parts of the Sardinian coast most heavily besieged by tourism, previously uninhabited because poorly equipped by nature (lack of water and fuel, lack of safe landing places, very harsh climatic conditions outside of the short summer) to support human settlement based on a subsistence economy such as agriculture, livestock farming or fishing; drawbacks which are easily overcome as a result of technological advances and, above all, of greater economic potential.

In the absence of any consolidated built context, there would seem to be a relaxation of any obligation to conform to stringent rules regarding volumes, typologies, materials and colours; nevertheless, even for architectures implanted in a natural setting, especially in an exceptional one, the relationship with the surroundings takes on special importance, influencing the final appearance of the project. Landscape and architecture, when they are forced into proximity with one another, can be mutually enriched or damaged, and while it is often true that the landscape can suffer beyond recognition as a result of new building, the wrong environmental context will inevitably ruin even an architecture of value.

It is not difficult to see that the architect can approach the relationship with the setting with attitudes that range from absolute respect to conscious rejection, depending on the natural characteristics of the context and the architect's philosophy. A strong architectural gesture will impose itself on its surroundings, and in extreme instances condition them, bending the environment to the demands of the new construction: one thinks of the sharp contrast between the natural disorder of the coastline and pure geometrical forms, the squared volumes of the rigorously rationalist villas of Daneri and Ponti.

In preference to these protagonistic houses, which stand out cleanly against the natural background, other architects have opted instead for fragmented houses, integrated into the natural setting, perhaps opening only towards the sea, and only visible from the sea, surrounded by rocks, hidden away amongst the dense Mediterranean vegetation.

There are many different ways of seeking a harmonious insertion into the landscape: in the house by Bicocchi & Monsani in Castiglione della Pescaia, the pine grove enters, indeed almost invades, the interior space, while the construction by Melluso & Ministeri in Villafranca Tirrena has served to introduce a new organic order into the different elements of the environment, to the point of arriving, as the antithesis of rationalist architecture, at organic architecture's most extreme experiments with the habitable sculpture designed by Couëlle. Integration with the environment has also been sought in the use of mimetic materials: in Cavallo, Larini & Rainieri chose enduring, natural materials which not only harmonize with their surroundings but require a minimum of maintenance; in Menghi's villa the colour of the walls is very close to that of the massive outcrops of granite scattered across the surrounding landscape; the house by Boeri at Punta Cannone is covered in its entirety in a plaster made with powdered local granite, as a means of giving the house the same constantly changing colour as the rocks.

On the coastline, too, the rapport between interior and exterior varies radically, depending on the climatic conditions and in relation to the problems of construction and of making life enjoyable for the inhabitants, particularly where this is a question of spending the summer in a place that is seasonally-occupied and not always adapted to human settlement. A great number of houses have a common approach to the "environmental" defence against the wind, the sea, the heat and the light. The solutions to these problems —resolved in other countries exclusively through the use of the appropriate technologies, (as in the abuse of air conditioning in the United States) —have, in many of the examples selected here, directly influenced the typology of the construction.

The external appearance may be profoundly marked by the presence of elements designed to filter and moderate the fierceness of the light, such as pergolas, porticoes and brise-soleil screens: one thinks of the villa designed by Studio Transit in Formia, with its entrances and windows protected from the sun by wooden grilles that are at once functional and decorative. Other architects shelter the interior spaces with thick walls, with narrow slits or even blind walls: one of the houses by Boeri in Sardinia, with an external form reminiscent of a bunker, stands out from the surrounding countryside, while the Bevilacqua house by Portoghesi recalls a fortress in its massive outward appearance, inspired by the labyrinthine complexity of the old towns. The separation/ diaphragm with the exterior created by the walls is quite sharp, and the house turns in on itself introspectively. It may open onto an interior courtyard or patio, as do the villa by Menghi on Elba or the other villa by Boeri in La Maddalena whose distribution, as in the house by Larini & Rainieri in Cavallo, tends to a great extent to resolve the problems of habitability created by the wind.

It is difficult, as matters stand, to avoid using an almost ritual disclaimer. The choice of these architectures has not been impartial, and obviously it reflects the taste and the logic of the authors. Nevertheless, without limiting themselves solely to those houses whose inspiration is based in the traditions of the Modern Movement, with which the authors feel most closely involved, space has been set aside for a variety of different experiences, the only exclusions being postmodern and pseudo-vernacular pastiche, amply represented in other publications.

This book is dedicated to those individuals —architects and clients— who have, in the midst of so much bad or indifferent architecture, successfully fought against the banal and the temptations of mannerism.

We deeply regret that we have been unable to include certain very interesting houses, because of a lack of photographic documentation, either originally deficient or adversely affected by time's passage, while new photographs could not be taken because the houses are now in a poor state of conservation, have been transformed by their owners, or simply hidden by vegetation that has grown up in the intervening years.

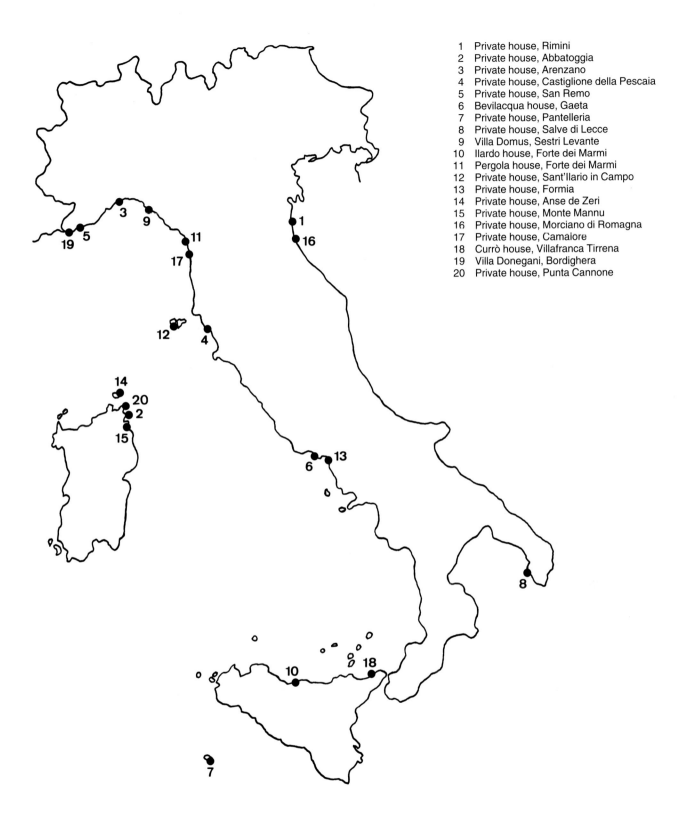

1 Private house, Rimini
2 Private house, Abbatoggia
3 Private house, Arenzano
4 Private house, Castiglione della Pescaia
5 Private house, San Remo
6 Bevilacqua house, Gaeta
7 Private house, Pantelleria
8 Private house, Salve di Lecce
9 Villa Domus, Sestri Levante
10 Ilardo house, Forte dei Marmi
11 Pergola house, Forte dei Marmi
12 Private house, Sant'Ilario in Campo
13 Private house, Formia
14 Private house, Anse de Zeri
15 Private house, Monte Mannu
16 Private house, Morciano di Romagna
17 Private house, Camaiore
18 Currò house, Villafranca Tirrena
19 Villa Donegani, Bordighera
20 Private house, Punta Cannone

# Private house

Annio Maria Matteini, architect
Rimini, Emilia-Romagna, 1983

The building stands in a qualitatively poor, ambiguous context, and the limited dimensions of the plot, the extremely restrictive planning regulations, the impossibility of seeing the sea –despite its great proximity– and the likelihood of the house being subdivided between the two sons in the near future all conditioned the architectural solution.

The primary form in this construction is a cube with a side of 10 metres, laid out over three floors. Symmetry and asymmetry are determined by the interplay of projecting and recessed volumes. The primary volume is eroded, revealing the structure coinciding with the entrance portico, the deep balconies, the spacious, two-dimensional closed areas that correspond to the linear windows.

The deep open spaces delimit a part of the ground floor directly communicating with the internal stairs. A second flight of stairs can be attached to the projecting triangular volume in the event of a subdivision of the building into two parts.

The succession of visual openings on each floor, related to the widening out of the corridors and to the alternately projecting and recessed balconies, thus constitutes an urban framework into which the elements of the internal spatial articulation are interlinked.

Plans, section, axonometric sketch and views of the exterior

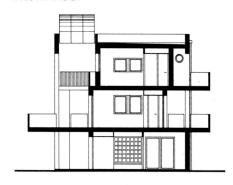

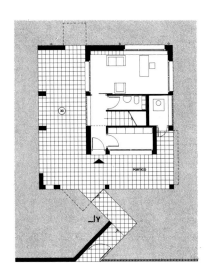

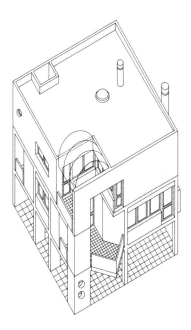

14

## Private house

Cini Boeri, architect
Abbatoggia, La Maddalena, Sardinia,1966-1967

Situated in the part of the island most exposed to the wind, the house stands out from the surrounding landscape. Rooted to the rocks that slope down to the sea, in external appearance the house recalls a bunker, while its interior spaces respect the natural differences in level of the site.

Shelter from the weather is provided by double walls with an air cavity, which link together the trapezoidal reinforced concrete spurs; the external rendering is made of cement and protected by a coating of epoxy resin.

In plan the house reveals itself as being composed of four apparently independent rooms, each with its own bathroom and access to the exterior, yet at the same time connecting with the central space consisting of kitchen and living room and the courtyard that opens towards the sea.

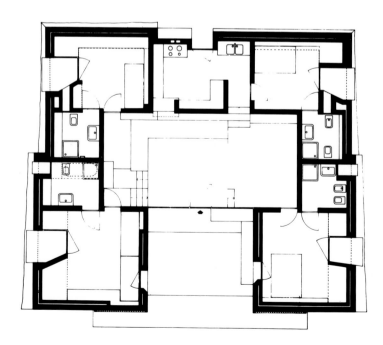

Plan and views of the exterior

19

# Private house

Vico Magistretti, architect
Arenzano, Liguria, 1963-1964

This house hidden away inside a pine wood had to be laid out on one level to comply with planning regulations.

This fact suggested appropriating part of the low roof as a terrace, conceived not simply as a belvedere enjoying an exceptionally fine view, but rather for use as a second living area, the same size as the first, and intended above all for taking advantage of the cool of the summer evenings.

Providing the link with the entrance, the gently inclined arched flight of stairs which runs between the two living areas is an architectonically powerful element, creating a short panoramic progression in a house that is not easy to read, somewhat confused and composed of asymmetries.

The living room in the centre of the building opens out onto the main portico, which turns to face the sea. Two wings are developed on either side of this, creating a clear separation between the service area and the family's living space, which is in turn divided into two and gravitates towards the large play area onto which the children's bedrooms open.

The dominant tones are white and black, determined by a choice of finishes and materials, such as slate, recalling those used in traditional Ligurian architecture.

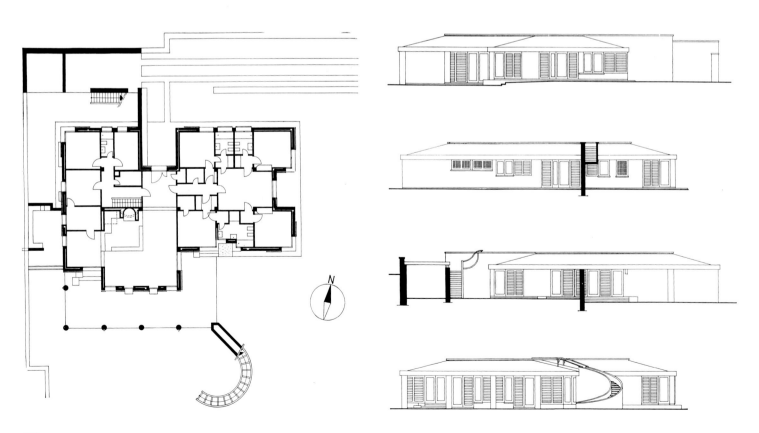

26

**Private house**
Giancarlo and Luigi Biccochi, Roberto Monsani, architects
engineer: Lisindo Baldassini
Pineta di Roccamare, Castiglione della Pescaia, Tuscany, 1974

Standing in the midst of the pine covered sea marsh, the house is revealed as an extended grid-like structure with a tubular steel framework and fixed panels.

Surrounded by the pines which it turns outwards to face, the spacious open sectors that separate the three volumes of the house are penetrated by the trees. The first of these volumes, for the use of guests, is clearly detached and distinct; the two others, which have minimal contact, accomodate the owners' bedrooms and the area for daytime use.

Designed in such a way as to allow the greatest possible flexibility to the different spaces, the house can be opened up completely in summer. All of the walls are identical square grids which form sliding partitions for the major part of their length, composed of opaque panels and panes of smoked glass; the movement of the sliding partitions gives the house a constantly changing floor plan, creating new spaces and new perspectives. The paving, of large wooden tiles, is the same inside and out, and the roof is constructed of overlapping self-supporting sheets of aluminium resting on the upper part of the tubular grid. The beds and other permanent furnishings were designed especially for the house.

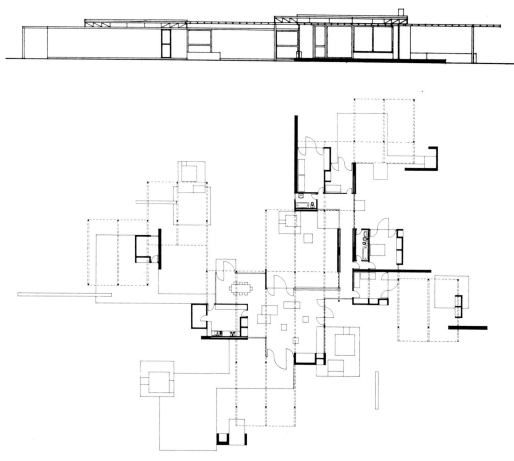

Plan, section and overall views showing the unity of house and landscape

# Private house

Bruno Sacchi, architect
San Remo, Liguria, 1979-1983

The architect took a single-storey villa dating from the early years of the century, subject to rigid planning restrictions which prohibited any volumetric modification, as the basis for this drastic intervention. The original roof has been replaced with a new structure consisting of four pairs of steel beams laid in a cross formation and joined together in such a way as to leave an opening for a skylight in the middle. Sections have been removed from the outer walls to form large irregular windows opening out onto terraces, one of which looks towards the sea.

The interior of the building, freed of supporting the weight of the roof, has been given more light by means of large openings in the original attic space, while a series of new floors on several different levels animates the extensive daytime zone and delimits the various areas.

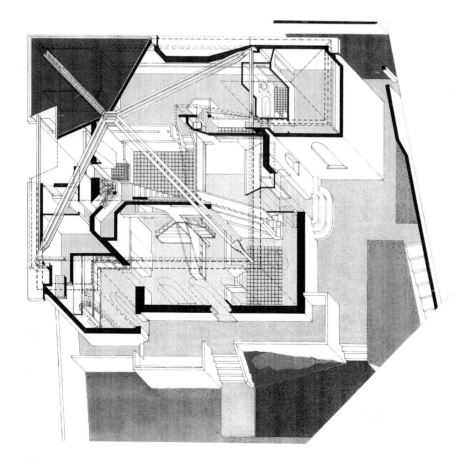

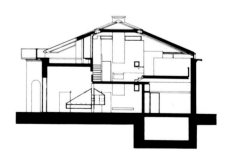

# Bevilacqua house

Paolo Portoghesi, Vittorio Gigliotti, architects
Gaeta, Lazio, 1966-1971

The villa, situated on a rocky promontory, draws its inspiration from the labyrinthine complexity of the urban layout of the old towns of southern Italy.

The massive quality of the house's external appearance is reminiscent of a fortress. The studied confusion of the often blind walls protects the interior spaces, which are organized in terms of a complicated ring-shaped geometric scheme: convex curves in the form of fragments of a spiral collide with the rectilinear elements constructed on an orthogonal grid.

The collision/conflict between these two clearly differentiated structures is underlined on the facades by the diversity of the materials employed: exposed reinforced concrete for the curvilinear walls, unrendered fair-faced brick for the rectilinear sections, and varnished concrete for the terraced roof, which recalls the complex movement of the load-bearing walls.

In the interior, the villa is laid out over two levels: the lower contains the daytime area, while the bedrooms are concentrated on the upper floor, continuing out onto terraces with views of the sea.

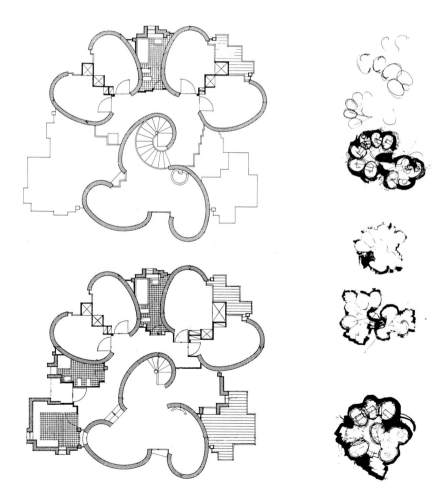

Plans, sketch and view of the house from the sea

# Private house

Oscar Tusquets and Lluís Clotet, architects
Cala di Tramontana, Island of Pantelleria, Sicily, 1972-1975

Olive trees, vines and junipers provide the setting for this house which Ignazio Gardella has described as "homeric".

The construction is articulated on two levels, which are laid out on the existing terracing of the fields. The bedrooms, and an open area for sunbathing screened from the wind by a semicircular wall, are concentrated on the upper level, which incorporates an old "dammuso", a typical agricultural construction of the region. The lower part of the house, on the other hand, is occupied by a single, irregular-shaped room which communicates with a terrace by way of a long strip of casement doors. Two staggered rows of pilasters, differing in number on the two levels, run parallel to the edges of the terraces. Some of these support the wooden beams which hold up the canopy that shades the terrace from the sun, while the others have no function other than the purely decorative.

The two Catalan architects have made use of elements, materials and finishes typical of the local architectonic tradition, spontaneously and powerfully influenced by the character of the place, such as the double pergola, the cladding in igneous stone and the pink and yellow rendering, and the roof in the form of a "dammuso" cupola.

Plans, section through the courtyard and view of the house and its surroundings

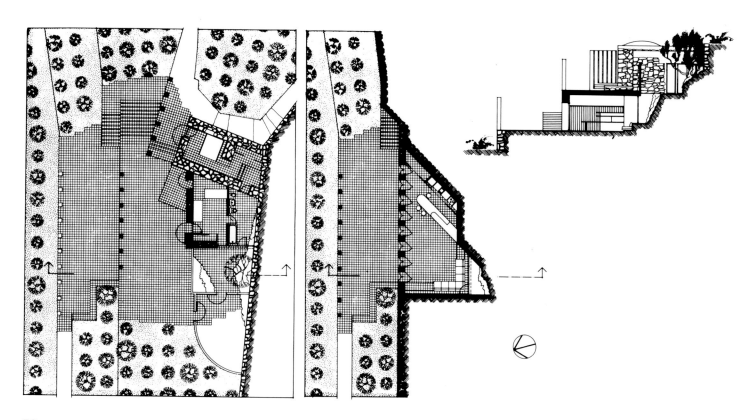

52

Sketch and various views of the exterior

Views of the interior of the ground
floor

# Private house

Alberto Salvati, Ambrogio Tresoldi, architects
Salve di Lecce, Puglia, 1982-1986

The intervention is situated within a small rural community at the southern tip of the Salentine peninsula. A series of independent volumes are grouped around a courtyard, conserving the typological and structural characteristics of the region's ancient settlements, dating back to the Greek colonies of the Cretan period. Each family dwelling unit was composed of four or five constructions: the "liame", which are residential buildings having a rectangular plan, barrel vaulting and thick walls of tufa, with an inclined outer facade; the "pagliare" for sheltering the livestock; the conical oven.

The buildings that make up the complex have been partially reconstructed, in part restored using traditional building methods and materials. The restored elements are distinguished by the exposed stone of their facades, while the reconstructed buildings have walls of rendered tufa blocks.

The architects have opted for a primary language composed of pure geometrical elements (pyramids, cubes, cylinders) laid out on plinths constructed of tufa, which rest in turn on the series of natural platforms which drop down to the nearby water course. Buildings, terraces and courtyards are articulated over a number of levels, following the contours of the terrain. One new building houses the living room-dining room, another a bedroom complete with bath, while the restored elements comprise the second nighttime area to the rear and the oven for baking bread. The scheme also includes the construction of an open-air kitchen, ringed and sheltered by walls pierced by openings that look out to the sea.

Plan, sections and views of the house and its surroundings

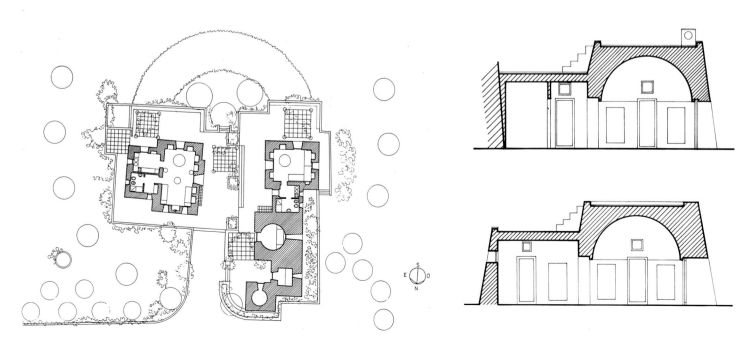

60

61

Views of the exterior and detail of
one of the terraces

## Villa Domus

Luigi Carlo Daneri, architect
restoration by Luciano Panero, architect
Sestri Levante, Liguria, 1936-1940/1980

This large villa was built on a stretch of coastline of rugged beauty, at the tip of a rocky peninsula, with a sheer drop to the sea below on one side, while on the landward side the terrain slopes gently down to form a valley. Despite the fact that this is a rigorously rationalist construction, the architect displays an exceptional sensitivity to the setting. Rising up from the clean horizontal lines of the terraces, the construction is laid out on the terrain in compliance with its changes of level. As a result, the house seems to comprise a single storey when seen from the west and from much of the seaward side, revealing four floors when seen from the east and two from the north. While the openings of windows and porticoes correspond to a desire to enjoy the best views of the surrounding panorama, the exterior form of the villa nevertheless reflects its internal layout. The problem of distribution has been resolved by dividing the interior space into three separate blocks, each with direct access to the main entrance. The block to the east contains the nighttime area: the owner's apartment (completely separate from the rest of the house), the guests' quarters on the floor above, and the servants' bedrooms on the entrance level. The southern block contains the large living room, while the third, westward, block houses the dining room, kitchen and services, laid out over two floors. After suffering modifications over the years, a sensitive and skilful restoration scheme has now given back to the villa its original rooms and detailing.

Plans, site plan, section and views of the exterior

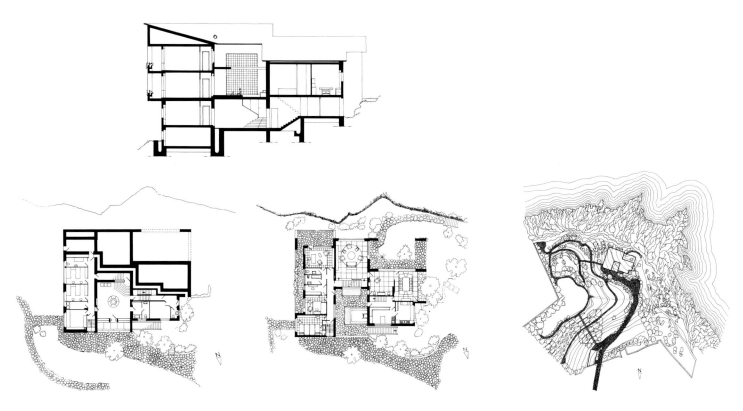

66

Detail of the external staircase and the access

## Ilardo house

Michele Beccu/Paolo Desideri/Filippo Raimondo, architects
Francesco Palamara/Francesco Portera, engineers
Piana Timpa, Lascari, Sicily, 1982-1984

The villa has been built next to an old rustic structure, on a steeply sloping site that enjoys panoramic views of the plain of Lascari and the sea. In addition to providing for seasonal visits by the family, the scheme derives from a desire to impose a more considered and rational order on the property's agricultural activity. The main concern was for the form of the house to reflect this dual function while putting forward a unitary response.

The composition of the building has taken account of the differences in level of the terrain. The house in fact tends to harmonize with the surrounding farmland, characterized by the terraces planted with citrus trees.

In planimetric terms the building is developed from east to west, on the basis of a longitudinal corridor with the various different rooms opening off it. The already existing volume is at the extreme western end of this passageway, with a pergola at the eastern end, and the garage beneath it. In keeping with the traditional layout of country houses in the region, a belvedere terrace runs the length of the north facade. Very little of the south facade projects above ground, and the only openings here are for service windows.

Plan, sections, elevation and views of the exterior

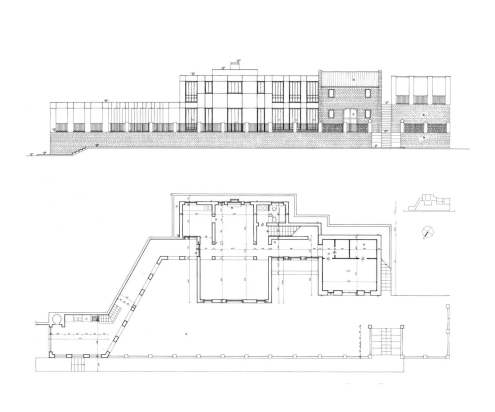

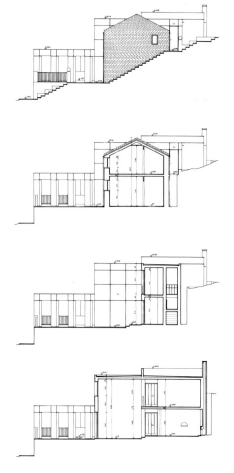

Various views and details of the
exterior

# Pergola house

Lorenzo Papi, architect
Forte dei Marmi, Tuscany, 1975-1976

The house stands in the Versilian countryside between the pine woods overlooking the sea and the first outcrops of the marble-whitened Apuan Alps, fitting in well with its surroundings, amidst the fields with their rhythmic succession of vines and trellisses, and reflects the traditional country-house layout in which the dining room (with its fireplace) is continued outwards to occupy a spacious area shaded by pergolas in summer.

The villa is composed of two separate nuclei: the daytime area occupies a central single-storey construction, while the nighttime area comprises two clearly distinct symmetrical volumes. These two parallel volumes communicate with the central part of the house by way of twin staircases in metal, wood and glass, forming between them two small courtyards covered by steel wires and pergolas supporting vines and awnings. The large solarium-terrace over the living room can be reached from the garden by way of two spiral staircases.

Plans, sections and views of the exterior

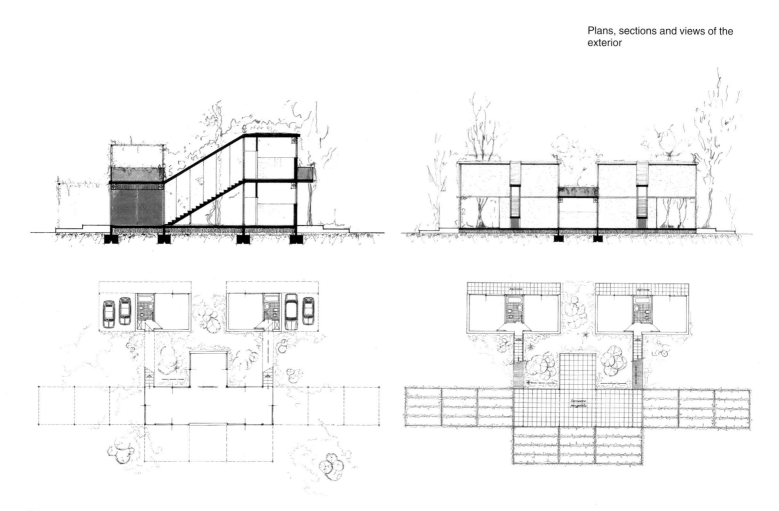

Views of the exterior and detail of
the stairs

86

# Private house

Roberto Menghi, architect
Sant'Ilario in Campo, Island of Elba, Tuscany, 1971-1973

The house stands on the side of the hill amidst dense undergrowth interspersed with vines, olives and fruit trees over the gentle slope of the terrain, adapting to the uneven contours of the site by means of slight changes in level. The building's height nowhere exceeds that of the "magazzini" which are found all over the island, built by the peasants to store their agricultural implements.

The colour of the walls recalls that of the outcrops of granite scattered in abundance across the terrain. The facades are rich in projecting and indented spaces and the resulting areas of light and shade which continue the *chiaroscuro* of the surrounding landscape.

At first sight the house has the look of an architecture closed in against the outside world, opening instead onto its central courtyard, but even the most internal areas of the house enjoy unexpected views of the countryside. Reached by means of a flight of stairs from the courtyard, the roof terrace is dotted with pyramidal volumes which correspond to the roofs of the rooms below. The openings in the tops of these serve for ventilation as well as providing a central skylight for the rooms below.

Plans, sections, elevations and views of the house and its surroundings

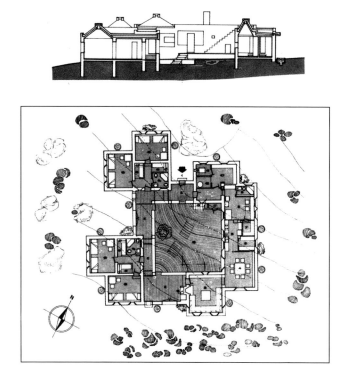

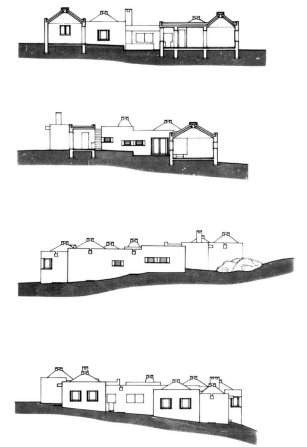

93

## Private house

Studio Transit (Giovanni Ascarelli/Maurizio Macciocchi/
Evaristo Nicolao/Danilo Parisio, architects).
Formia, Lazio, 1979-1982

Designed for a single family, the villa is nevertheless structured in two distinct living units, in two "generation" zones which enjoy complete functional autonomy within a single volume.

The extremely heterogeneous and confused architectonic context prompted the architects to isolate their building, protecting it behind a continuous high wall, leaving open only the stretch looking out on the bay of Gaeta.

The boundary wall is here a significant element within the architectural project: a subtle, sinuous band that follows the outline of the plot before penetrating into its heart to reach the house at its two lateral entrances.

The walls then extend into the interior of the building, creating a gallery which runs the full length of the house, connecting the various different rooms both horizontally and vertically. The rooms in fact open onto the gallery, which contains a series of balconies and suspended corridors that are visible from the different levels of the house, thus multiplying its visual depth.

The doors and windows are shaded from the sun by thick grilles of cedar wood; these elements, at once decorative and functional, are repeated in and modulate the interior.

The colours used on the outside of the house cover a chromatic scale that ranges from the Mediterranean white of the main volume, through the light grey of the boundary wall to the dark grey of the cylinders of the stairways and the chimneys.

Plans, sections and view of the exterior

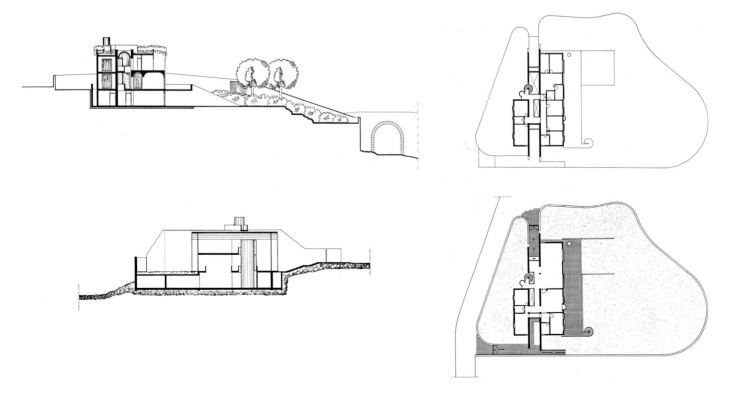

Detail of the perimeter wall and the garden facade

98

# Private house

Silvano and Simone Larini, Giovanna Rainieri, architects
extension: Giovanni Drago, architect
Anse de Zeri, Cavallo, Sardinia, 1986

The villa stands on a narrow finger of rock, virtually surrounded by the sea, at the mouth of the Bocche di Bonifacio. The problems of habitability posed by the winds were resolved by exploiting the topography of the terrain, which suggested the creation of two sea-facing terraces on opposite sides of the villa, for use at different times according to whether the wind is blowing from west or east. The large windows of the living room and dining room look onto this exterior space. The rooms in the interior are articulated with slight changes in level, which follow the contours of the plot. The durable natural materials were chosen with a view to harmonizing with the house's surroundings as well as requiring minimum maintenance.

Plan, perspective and view of the exterior

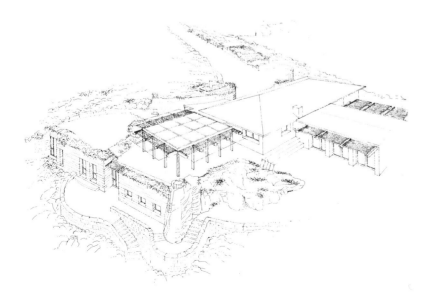
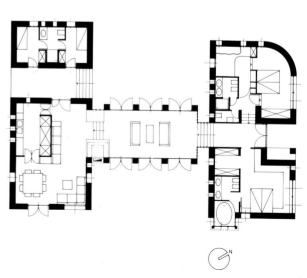

Views of the interior and of the
terraces

## Private house

Jacques Couëlle, architect
Monte Mannu, Costa Smeralda, Sardinia, 1966

At the opposite end of the spectrum from rationalist architecture, this habitable sculpture was designed with particular concern for its harmonious integration into the landscape. In every detail, the house reflects the philosophy of its architect: "The right angle does not exist in nature. The perfectly straight line does not exist in human behaviour."

Standing on a sloping site covered with the typical maquis underbrush of the Mediterranean, the house's exterior walls twist in and out of the juniper trees, which have all been conserved. The outer walls are clad with a mosaic of irregular multicoloured tiles, in which blue predominates, and this cladding extends, following the contours of the terrain, to the swimming pool cut out of the rock of the cliff overlooking the sea.

A terraced structure characterizes the entire project: from the garden, laid out on three distinct levels, to the interior of the house, where every room is on a different level.

Both inside and outside, irregular forms predominate, and only specially commissioned furniture fits the rooms here, with their surprising shapes. All of the walls and ceilings are exuberantly modelled and decorated, with inserts of glass, ceramic and terracotta. In addition, the architect has employed natural local materials, ranging from untreated wood to megalithic slabs of pink and grey granite, in unusual ways.

The enormous living room, 20 metres long, is the central space of the house, and opens out towards the sea and the waterfall in the garden.

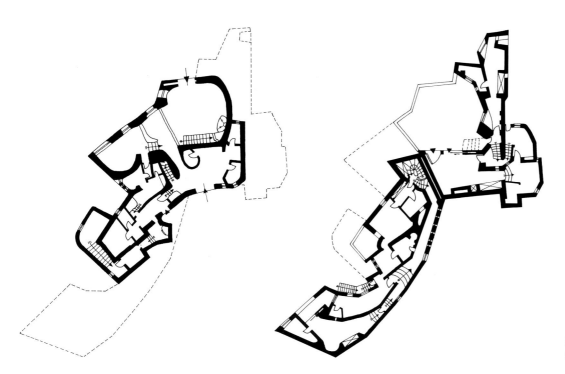

Plans, view of the access and of the swimming pool

# Private house
Annio Maria Matteini, architect
Morciano di Romagna, Emilia-Romagna, 1981

Although situated in one of the largest tourist resorts in Italy, the villa stands in a peripheral zone lacking in quality, and avoids making reference to its immediate vicinity. Nevertheless, the deep portico is perhaps evocative of a traditional typological feature of the region's rural houses.

The scheme here is articulated around an open space, central to the architectural composition, which is defined by means of three different-sized elementary volumes. The central space, virtually a courtyard as a continuation of the portico, is delimited by a C-shaped construction consisting of two orthogonally positioned volumes and a third, free-standing volume separated by a narrow vertical fissure which emphasizes the functional independence of the two parts of the house. The main volume is laid out over two floors, with the bedrooms on the ground floor, communicating directly with the garden, while the living room on the first floor opens onto a solarium-terrace. The upper floor of the services volume contains the smaller apartment, which is reached by way of an external staircase leading up from the portico.

The prevalence, in formal terms, of wall surfaces is underlined by the use of a pigment-free rendering whose irregular finish gives the building's exterior its particular character, deliberately creating a sense of something unfinished that is vaguely brutalist.

Plans, section and views of the exterior

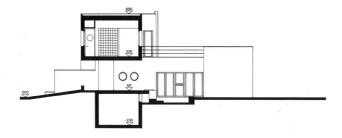

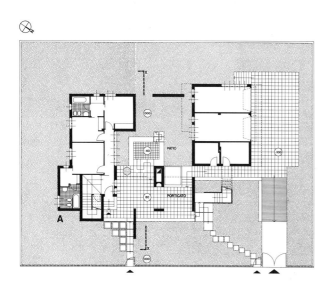

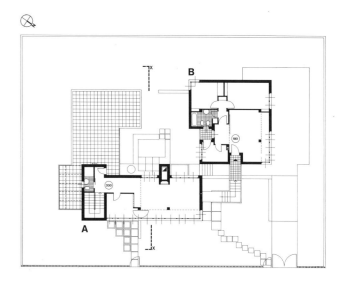

Views of the exterior and detail of
the skylight over the staircase

**Private house**
Lorenzo Papi, architect
with Ahmed Hadj Mourad, architect
Camaiore, Tuscany, 1989-1991

The architect has defined this villa as being on the one hand a *belvedere architecture,* thanks to its magnificent position, and on the other hand an *ornothological architecture,* as an expression of his great interest in seabirds. The roof of the house has been conceived in the form of the wings of two seagulls flying together, one a little higher than the other, to the sea. According to the architect, the house's occupants are able to live on one wing of the lower of the two seagulls, spread out in the sun, and at the same time under the partial shelter of the wings of the higher-flying seagull. These two pairs of wings (in white concrete, extremely light and slender) are the source of the idea of a villa that seems almost about to take off, resting lightly on the ground, without foundations.

Plans, section and views of the exterior

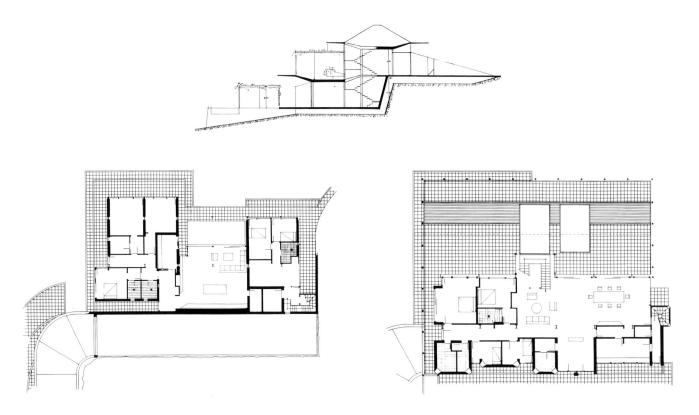

Views of the bedroom and living
room

125

# Curró house

Vicenzo Melluso, architect;
with Michele Ministeri, engineer.
Villafranca Tirrena, Sicily, 1981-1982

The main objective of the architect was to involve all of the existing elements (the palm trees, the citrus grove, the road flanked by the boundary walls, the water, the sky) in the implanting – by means of the conversion of an isolated agricultural building – of the new residential use, and to introduce a new organic order to the different parts of the terrain. The house, with its four facades, at once divides and unifies the exterior spaces, which have conserved their original diversity of morphologies and uses. The entrance to the property leads in, by way of the garden of palm trees and pools, to the public rooms of the house. On the far side the kitchen opens onto the walled orchard of citrus trees. The wall of the facade facing the road has expanded, doubling the height of the old wall built to contain the terrace and the length of the house's front facade.

Plan, elevations, sketch and view of the street facade

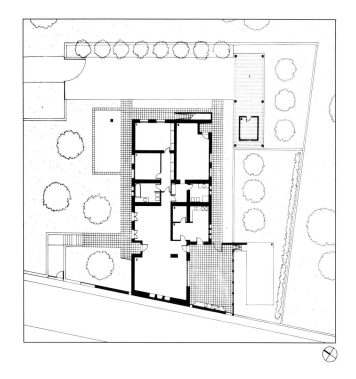

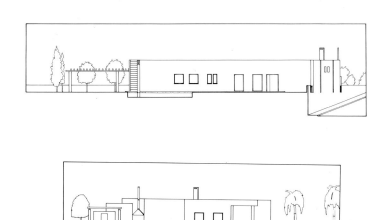

128

Views of the exterior from the
garden and detail of the external
staircase

## Villa Donegani

Giò Ponti, architect
restoration by Piero Pinto, architect
Bordighera, Liguria, 1935-1936/1981

The villa, surrounded by a luxuriant growth of palms, stands out as a clean, square white volume interrupted by the pure geometrical forms of the large windows.

Ponti designed the villa in such a way that even the innermost rooms enjoyed views of the sea, but over the years his original project underwent considerable modification. Ponti's drawings, perhaps due to the fact that many of the decisions were made by the architect on site, have not been found, and this has allowed greater freedom of expression to the restructuring project. Although the renovation of the facade has opted for reopening the portholes and "bands" of windows that were such typical features of the rationalist architecture of the period, the approach adopted in the interior was to undertake a decisive reorganization of the various spaces. The two floors, originally quite distinct, have been brought into communication with one another; the new living room is twice the height of the original one, and leaves the staircase connecting the two floors exposed to view. The living room has been provided with a large new window on the facade that overlooks the marina; to the right a stepping-back of the facade has created a roofed courtyard; to the left, on the far side of the dining room, is a small open courtyard with an olive tree in the centre.

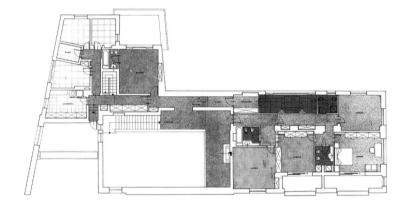

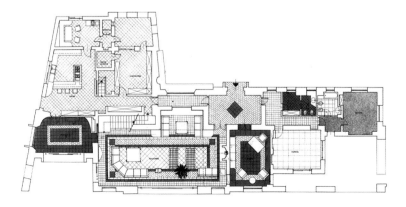

Plans and view of the exterior from the sea

Various views of the exterior

Views of the swimming pool and the porch

# Private house

Cini Boeri, architect
Punta Cannone, La Maddalena, Sardinia, 1966-1967

Huddled amongst the rocks carved by the fierce winds that blow from the Bocche de Bonifacio, this house stands on its own on a stretch of coast of extraordinary natural beauty. The rooms have been laid out in a ring around a circular courtyard, sheltered from the wind, which acts as the articulation between the two independent zones of the family apartment, with the services, and the guests' apartment.

The architect has sought to root the villa in the landscape, carefully positioning it on the steeply sloping site and treating the exterior with a render mixed with powdered local granite in order to give the house the same constantly changing colour as the surrounding rocks. The central nature of the courtyard is further underlined chromatically by the white concrete of the terraces.

Plan, section and view of the courtyard

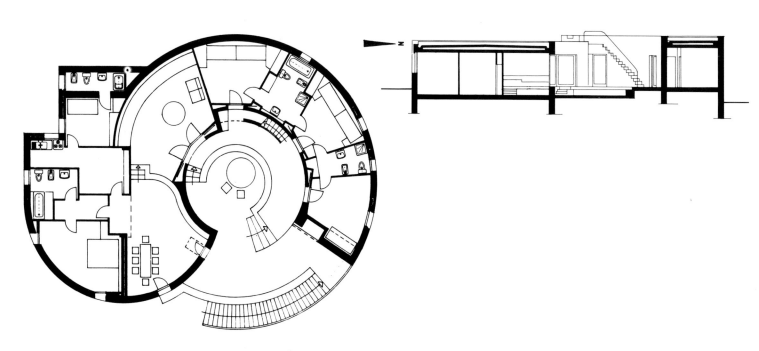

Various views of the exterior and the courtyard

141

# Photographers

Gabriele Basilico: pp. 113, 114, 115, 116, 117

Aldo Ballo: pp. 53, 56, 57, 58, 59

Carla de Benedetti: pp. 23, 24, 25, 26, 27, 28, 29, 31, 32, 33, 34, 35, 37, 38, 39, 40, 41, 68, 69, 70 (superiores), 71, 72, 73, 76, 77, 83, 84, 85, 86, 87, 89, 90, 91, 92, 93, 131, 132, 133, 134, 135, 136, 137

Crimella: pp. 67, 70 (inferior), 74, 75

Jacopo Faggioni: pp. 140, 141

Giancarlo Gardin: pp. 103, 104, 105, 106, 107, 109, 110, 111

Giovanna Piemonti: pp. 95, 96, 97, 98, 99, 100, 101

Nuccio Rubino: pp. 127, 128, 129

Benvenuto Saba: pp. 119, 120, 121, 122, 123, 124, 125

Laura Salvati: pp. 61, 62, 63, 64, 65